Mythical Beasts

MYTHICAL MONSTERS

By Joanne Rippin

Cavendish Square

Published in 2023 by Cavendish Square Publishing, LLC
2544 Clinton Street, Buffalo, NY 14224

Originally Published in English by Haynes Publishing under the title: *Mythical Beasts Pocket Manual* © Haynes Publishing 2020

Website: cavendishsq.com

Design and layout by Richard Parsons
Thanks to the following agencies for use of their images:
Alamy; (cover) pp 24, 30. **Bridgeman Art Library;** pp 13, 14. **Getty;** p 28.
Shutterstock Grom08 (cover).

Cataloging-in-Publication Data

Names: Rippin, Joanne.
Title: Mythical monsters / Joanne Rippin.
Description: New York : Cavendish Square Publishing, 2023. | Series: Mythical beasts | Includes glossary and index.
Identifiers: ISBN 9781502667274 (pbk.) | ISBN 9781502667281 (library bound) | ISBN 9781502667298 (ebook)
Subjects: LCSH: Animals, Mythical--Juvenile literature. | Mythology--Juvenile literature.
Classification: LCC GR825.R577 2023 | DDC 398.24'54--dc23

CPSIA compliance information: Batch #CWCSQ23: For further information contact Cavendish Square Publishing LLC at 1-877-980-4450.

Printed in the United States of America

The Author

Joanne is an experienced writer and editor who has published many historical books on a wide variety of subjects. She has a long-standing fascination with mythical creatures and has a dog who thinks it's half human.

Contents

BASILISK
LETHAL KING OF SERPENTS

The basilisk was a mythical beast that the Greeks believed was native to the country of Libya. A Roman author named Pliny the Elder described it as a small snake, "not more than 12 fingers in length." Other authors said a basilisk was born when a rooster sat on a snake's egg. It had a crested head and was so venemous that it could kill its victims simply with a touch, breath, or even look. One legend said that when a knight stabbed a basilisk with his lance, the venom traveled up the spear's shaft and killed the knight. The basilisk's mortal enemy was the weasel.

FROM BASILISK TO COCKATRICE

By the 11th and 12th centuries, the basilisk had become a much larger creature, with fiery breath and a deadly cry. It was now called a cockatrice, and it had a rooster's head, neck, and legs. Some versions had dragon's wings, too. It could turn people to stone with one look, and its breath would wither fruit on a tree. The cockatrice became used as a symbol in heraldry in the 14th and 15th centuries.

BASILISK

Did you know?

The Romans believed that the Sahara desert was created by a basilisk burning up the grasses and trees that had once grown there.

Safety Tips for Travelers

People in medieval times really believed that cockatrices existed. Travelers who had to pass through Libya were given advice on how to stay safe. One method of protection was to carry mirrors to reflect the creature's deadly gaze back onto itself. Another was to travel with a weasel, which would chase and even kill a cockatrice, or a rooster, as the cockatrice would have a deadly fit if it heard the rooster crow. Were these "safety" tips actually made up by cunning salesmen taking advantage of nervous travelers in a new country?

Known Facts

Name:	Basilisk, later cockatrice
Family status:	The basilisk came from a snake's egg hatched by a rooster; the cockatrice came from a rooster's egg hatched by a snake or toad
Career:	Creating deserts, killing people with their deadly gaze
Personality:	Scared of nothing except for weasels and roosters
Appearance:	Originally a snake; later a creature that was half dragon, half rooster

How to stop a cockatrice from hatching

A cockatrice was born from an egg that had been laid by a rooster and incubated by a snake or toad. It was said that if you spotted the unnatural act of a male chicken actually laying an egg, you should quickly pick it up and throw it over your house. If it landed on the other side without touching the house, the cockatrice wouldn't hatch.

Bunyip

Australian Swamp Creature

This mysterious beast is rarely seen but is believed to live in the deserted swamps and marshes of Australia. In the dead of night, a bunyip's blood-curdling, booming roars can be heard for miles. It has a reputation for eating people, especially women and children. It is said to cause floods if its lair is disturbed. There are lots of different descriptions of what the bunyip looks like. Some say it is like a hairy hippopotamus. Others say it looks like many different animals put together. It may have scales, fur, fangs, or flippers.

Dreaming the Bunyip

Indigenous Australian people tell of the bunyip in their Dreamtime stories. According to one of these, the bunyip was once a tribesman who broke some rules and was banished as a punishment. Furious, the man became an evil spirit who roamed the waterways at night, bringing unhappiness and fear, and devouring everyone he met.

Did you know?

The bunyip is such a famous and important part of Australian mythology that in 1994, a set of four postage stamps was released, featuring different paintings of the creature.

REAL MARSUPIAL?

During the 19th century, people really believed the bunyip existed, and white colonizers in Australia claimed to have spotted them in marshes, lakes, and rivers. In 1890, Melbourne Zoo tried (and failed) to catch a bunyip that had been sighted several times near Victoria. In more recent times, historians have suggested that the Indigenous descriptions of the bunyip may have come from a large, now-extinct marsupial called Diprotodon. It was as big as a hippopotamus—the largest marsupial ever to have lived.

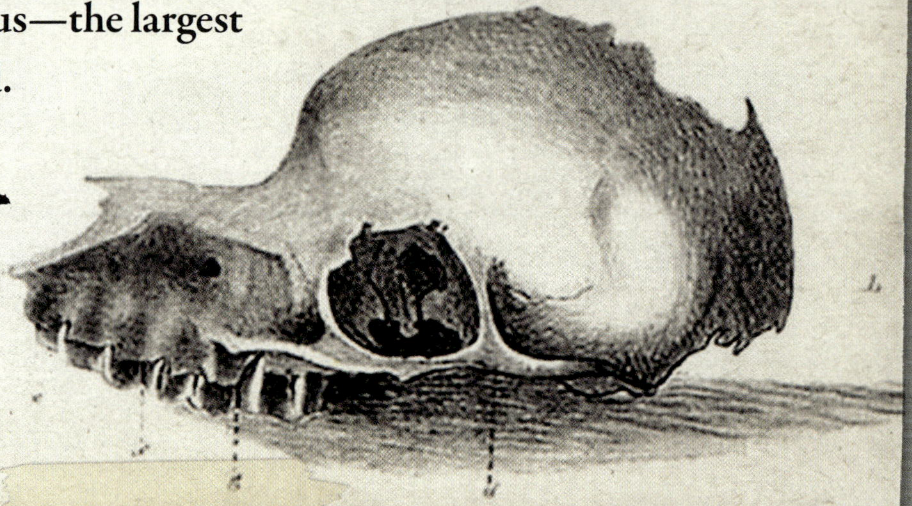

The person who found this deformed calf's skull in 1846 believed it to be a bunyip's skull.

Known Facts

Name:	Bunyip
Family status:	Perhaps a transformed human, perhaps an ancient giant marsupial
Career:	Lives in water, frightens humans with terrible roars
Personality:	Fierce and likely to attack, especially if its lair is under threat
Appearance:	Large and aquatic; all other descriptions vary widely

The bunyip and Goondah

One of the Dreamtime stories about the bunyip tells of a man called Goondah, who was fishing for eels when he accidentally caught one of the bunyip's cubs. In revenge, the furious bunyip changed Goondah into a swan.

CERBERUS

HUGE THREE-HEADED DOG

Cerberus is a mythical creature from ancient Greece. He is a monstrous dog with three heads and a snake for a tail. His eyes flash fire, and his three sets of jaws all have fanged teeth and, some say, three tongues. Some sources say that snake heads grow out of his fur. His parents were Typhon and Echidna (mother and father of so many of the mythical beasts of Greece), and he belonged to Hades, the Greek god of the underworld who set Cerberus to guard its entrance. If any of the dead tried to leave the underworld, the dog would eat them. He also prevented any of the living from entering. Although fierce, Cerberus was devoted and loyal to his master and was said to be fond of Persephone (wife of Hades). He was said to be gentle and even welcoming to new arrivals to the world of the dead.

FLUFFY

One of the beasts in JK Rowling's Harry Potter series is a three-headed dog. The dog, which belongs to Hagrid, has quite a few other similarities with Cerberus. He is loyal to his master and sticks to his task of guarding the entrance to a secret underground hiding place. The way to get past Fluffy is to play music until he falls asleep, and (according to Hagrid, anyway) he isn't fierce and deadly, but has a gentle, affectionate nature.

Hades, Persephone, and Cerberus

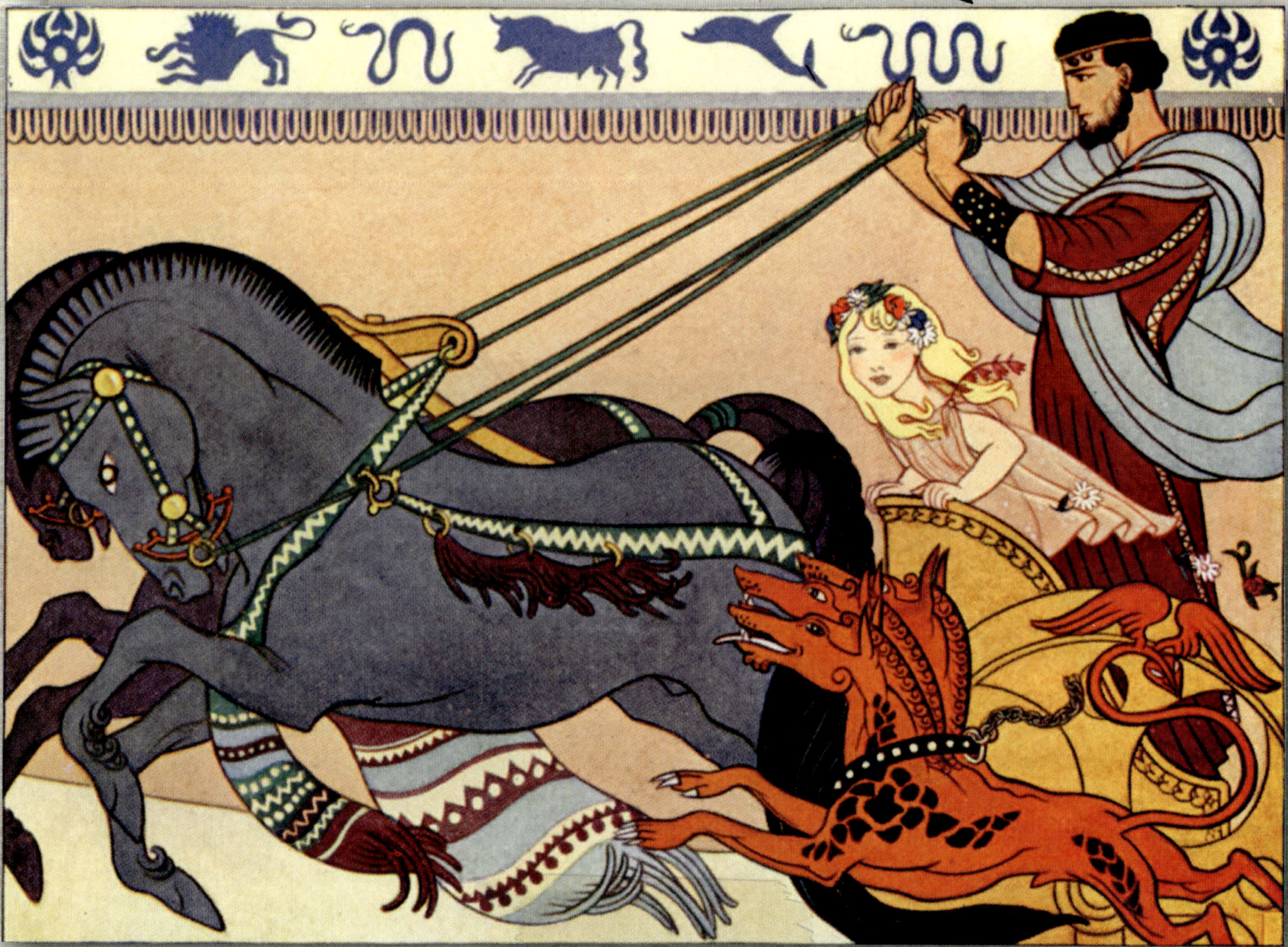

Did you know?

Cerberus's hearing was so acute, it was said he could hear the movement of ghosts.

Defeating Cerberus

The first time Cerberus is overcome is when Orpheus enters the underworld to find his wife and plays such an irresistible lullaby on his lute that Cerberus falls deeply asleep. Next came Hercules, who had been ordered to bring Cerberus out into the world of the living. Hades gave Hercules permission to do this, but only if he could capture the dog without using any of his weapons. Even though he was savagely bitten by the snake at the end of the dog's tail, Hercules dragged him out of the world of the dead. At the edge of the underworld, specks of foam that had spattered from Cerberus's snapping jaws took root and grew into the deadly poisonous aconite plant. The only other time Cerberus was defeated was when Aeneas entered the underworld, and got past Cerberus by feeding him a drugged honey cake.

Known Facts

Name:	Cerberus
Family status:	Father was Typhon, mother was Echidna, Hades is owner
Career:	Totally dedicated to his task of guarding the gate to the underworld
Personality:	Devoted and loyal to Hades, fierce, deadly
Appearance:	Three heads, sharp teeth, possibly nine tongues, huge shaggy body, and a serpent-headed tail

Why three heads?

Some people think that Cerberus's three heads represent birth, adulthood, and old age, while others think the heads have the ability to see into the past, present, and future.

MINOTAUR

BODY OF A MAN, HEAD OF A BULL

In ancient Greece, the queen of Crete gave birth to a son who was half human, half bull. As he grew older, he became fierce and uncontrollable, with a taste for human flesh. The queen's husband, King Minos, imprisoned him in a labyrinth underneath the city. The king and queen's other son, who was completely human, was later killed in the Greek city of Athens. As compensation, Minos demanded that every year the Athenians should send 14 of their young men and women as sacrificial food for the monster, now known as the Minotaur. Theseus, prince of Athens, chose to be part of the group of young people one year, and with the help of Ariadne, Minos's daughter, he killed the Minotaur.

Religious bulls

Ancient Egyptians worshipped a goddess named Hathor, who also had the head of a cow and the body of a human. Apis was a holy bull who was sometimes said to be Hathor's son.

Did you know?

Asterion, the Minotaur's real name, means "star." Some ancient Cretan coins have an engraving of a labyrinth on them, with a star in the center.

The Bulls of Knossos

Bulls play an important part in the myths of Crete. The animal that was said to have fathered the Minotaur was a white bull of unmatched beauty, which had been sent to King Minos by the god Poseidon. Many ancient images of bulls have been found in Crete's ancient remains, and it looks as if the animal was important in Cretan customs and beliefs. A fresco from Knossos, as the Cretan palace is now called, shows a young man leaping over the back of a huge bull. This suggests that there was some kind of ceremonial dance, or sport, that involved acrobats and a bull—a bit like the Spanish tradition of bullfighting. Perhaps it was to appear in this ceremonial event that the young people of Athens came to Crete, not as food for a mythical creature.

One of the bull frescoes at the palace of Knossos

Known Facts

Name:	Minotaur ("bull of Minos")
Family status:	Father was a magnificent white sacrificial bull; mother was Pasiphae, queen of Crete
Career:	His birth name was Asterion, and he was raised in the palace until he became too fierce to live with humans
Personality:	Wild, uncontrollable, more bull than human as he got older
Appearance:	The head and tail of a bull on a man's body
Symbols:	The labyrinth, a star

Only one Minotaur

Creatures called minotaurs have been used in fairy tales and paintings for centuries, and later in movies and video games. However, really there was only ever one—the half-bull prince of Crete.

VAMPIRE

IMMORTAL, HALF-BAT BLOODSUCKER

While more human than beast, a vampire is able to shift into other shapes, in particular that of a bat. Legends of vampires have existed for thousands of years, and there are stories of demonic bloodsucking spirits from ancient Mesopotamia, Judaea, and Greece. The folklore we know today, however, comes from Eastern Europe, particularly from the region of Transylvania, where the most famous vampire of all, Count Dracula, is from.

European Vampire Traditions

Folktales about vampires started in the 18th century in Romania and were so convincing that people began believing vampires really existed. Despite the fact that many myths and legends were dying out at this time, belief in vampires grew to a point where sightings were being reported to local priests and governments, and there were even official investigations. People believed that a vampire was a dead human who would rise up from their grave at night, and the only way to stop them was to exhume the body during the day and hammer a stake through the corpse's heart.

Did you know?

Vampires can't see their image in a mirror, and they cast no shadow. They can't eat any food other than blood, die if caught in direct sunlight, and can be repelled by holy water and crucifixes.

DRACULA AND NOSFERATU

Bram Stoker's story *Dracula* was published in 1897. It is the basis of most of our vampire legends today, including many books, movies, and TV series. Count Dracula lives in an isolated castle in Transylvania but wants to transport his body in its coffin to England in order to find new blood and spread his undead curse. His plans are stopped by Van Helsing and Jonathan and Mina Harker, who eventually hunt him down and destroy him. In 1922, a movie based on Stoker's novel was released called *Nosferatu: A Symphony of Horror*, with the name of the vampire changed to avoid copyright issues. Bram Stoker's heirs sued the film company, however, and won their case. It is thought that Stoker based the character of Dracula on a historical ruler of Wallachia (now in Romania) named Vlad III or Vlad the Impaler, son of Vlad Dracul.

Vlad III

Known Facts

Name: Vampire, vampyre, the undead

Family status: Vampires are created by other vampires who feed on their blood

Career: Live forever, sleep in their coffins during daylight hours, hunt for victims at night; can change into bats, climb walls, and are very strong

Personality: Mostly evil, cruel, and selfish, but in some stories capable of love and compassion, and even a desire to change

Appearance: Varies: sometimes ancient and skeletal, usually deadly pale with dark-rimmed eyes, red lips, and fanged teeth; sometimes superhumanly beautiful or handsome

Symbols: Fangs, bats, black cloaks

WEREWOLF

A HUMAN WHO TURNS INTO A WOLF

Myths and folk tales about "*were-*" creatures come from all over the world, and werewolves are the most common. *Were* is an Old English word for "man," and there are stories of werecats and weretigers as well as werewolves. The Roman poet Ovid tells one of the earliest tales of a werewolf, saying that Zeus punished a king called Lycaon by turning him into a bloodthirsty wolf with shaggy hair, red eyes, and a fierce human face.

MEDIEVAL WEREWOLVES

In medieval Europe, it was believed that transformation into a werewolf was linked to a full moon. In Russia, it was thought that a child born on Christmas Eve was in danger of becoming a werewolf. In Portugal, it was the seventh-born son who was at risk, so he was often named "Bento," meaning "blessed," as protection.

Werewolves vs. vampires

The ancient Greeks believed werewolves could turn into vampires after they died if their bodies weren't gotten rid of properly. In modern stories, werewolves are often shown as being the enemies of vampires. Some examples of this can be seen in Stephanie Meyer's Twilight series, in the movie *What We Do in the Shadows*, and in the video game *Underworld*.

Criminal Werewolves

In 15th- and 16th-century Europe, a few well-known criminals defended their horrible murders by claiming that at night they turned into werewolves and lost control. These cases may be explained by a very rare condition that was discovered much later. It was named lycanthropy after King Lycaon. This is a mental illness that causes people to believe they really do have the power to turn into a wolf.

Known Facts

Name:	Werewolf
Family status:	Humans that have been bitten by another werewolf
Career:	Can live normal lives until the night of a full moon, when they go on killing sprees
Personality:	When in wolf form, they are wild, savage, and uncontrollable
Appearance:	Like a regular wolf, or with a hairy human body and the head of a wolf

Did you know?

Norse legends spoke of shapeshifters who could turn into wolves if they covered themselves with the pelt, or skin, of a wolf. Viking warriors would often wear wolf pelts in battle to scare their enemies by suggesting they might transform at any moment.

YETI

FIERCE AND MYSTERIOUS CREATURE

Also known as the Abominable Snowman, the yeti is another mythical beast that people have told stories about for centuries. The yeti is said to live in the mountainous regions of Russia, China, and Nepal, and there are many stories of it being glimpsed faintly through swirling snowstorms. It sometimes leaves huge human-like tracks in the snow—some of which have been photographed. Despite dozens of expeditions into the remote mountain regions of the Himalayas, however, the existence of the yeti still hasn't been proved. In Nepal, parents used the yeti as a warning to children not to stray too far from home.

Yeti footprint, 1951

Yeti Stats

Based on the footprints, there have been some quite precise estimates on how tall and heavy the yeti might be. It is said to stand on two legs and is covered from head to toe with shaggy hair. It weighs between 200 and 400 pounds (91 and 181kg) and averages about 6 feet (1.8m) in height. In folktales, a yeti is an enormous, hairy, ape-like hominoid with huge feet and aggressive saber-like teeth. Its fur is either a red-brown, gray, or white color. Some of the fragments of bone or fur that have been brought back by expeditions looking for yetis have had DNA analysis that shows them to be from Himalayan brown bears.

Sasquatch

Some Native American cultures also have a kind of yeti. They call theirs Bigfoot or Sasquatch. It is a hairy, upright-walking, ape-like creature that lives in the forests of North America. It is said to be dangerous to humans who wander into its territory.

SHERPAS AND THE YETI

The Sherpa people are one of the ethnic groups who live in the most mountainous regions of Nepal and the Himalayas. Sherpas have a strong connection with stories of yeti sightings. They believe that yetis have brown fur and that their feet point backwards (toes at the back) to help them walk up hills better. The famous climber Sir Edmund Hillary led an expedition to hunt for the yeti in 1960 and found several brown, furry pelts. Other mountaineers, including Tenzing Norgay and Eric Shipton, have photographed yeti tracks high in the peaks. Yeti hunting became so popular that the U.S. embassy in Nepal gave out a list of rules in 1959. It said that people had to buy Yeti-hunting permits for $77. They could only kill a Yeti if they were in danger, and they had to give the government of Nepal any photographs they took of the creature.

Known Facts

Name:	Yeti, Abominable Snowman
Family status:	There are male and female yetis and they have children in the same way as humans do
Career:	Sherpas believe they steal crops and like drinking alcohol, but mostly they hide out of sight
Personality:	Fierce and may attack humans, but would probably just rather not be seen
Appearance:	A hybrid primate/hominoid with shaggy hair all over its face and body, sharp teeth, and large feet

Did you know?

A villager from a Sherpa village claimed to have been kidnapped by a yeti. He said that they like to eat frogs from mountain streams and enjoy throwing stones!

Glossary

acute: Very strong and sensitive.

exhume: To dig up a grave.

heraldry: The practice of tracing and recording family history and creating coats of arms.

hominoid: A primate of a group that includes humans, their fossil ancestors, and the anthropoid apes.

incubate: To sit upon eggs to hatch them by warmth.

Indigenous: The native people of an area, or something that belongs to them.

labyrinth: Maze.

lethal: Deadly.

For More Information

Krensky, Stephen, and Pham Quang Phuc. *The Book of Mythical Beasts and Magical Creatures.* New York, NY: DK Publishing, 2020.

Kiddle: Bunyip Facts for Kids. *https://kids.kiddle.co/Bunyip.*

Index